ABC's para ti

This book belongs

to:

A

Ant

Hormiga

B

Bee

Abeja

Dog

Perro

D

E

Elephant

Elefante

G

Giraffe

Jirafa

H

Hippopotamus
Hipopótamo

J

Jellyfish

Medusa

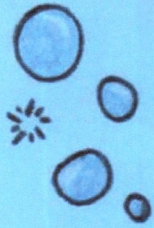
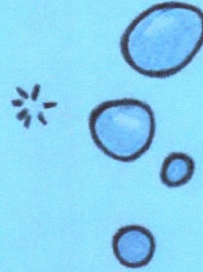
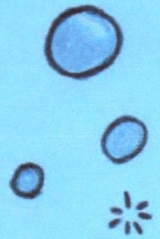

K

Kitten

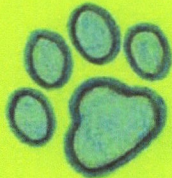

Gatito

Lion   León

L

M

Monkey

Mono

Newt   Tritón

N

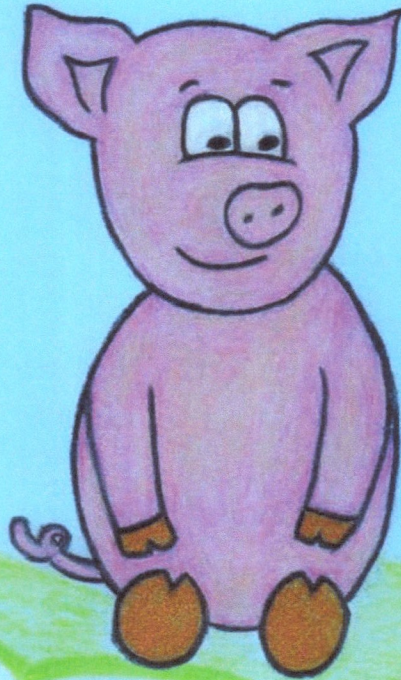

Queen Snake

Q

Serpiente Reina

Rabbit

R

Conejo

S

Sheep

Oveja

Turtle

T

Tortuga

U

Unicorn

Unicornio

V

Vulture

Buitre

W

Whale

Ballena

X

X-Ray Fish

Pez Rayos-X

Y

Yak

Yak

Z

Zebra

Cebra

Thank you!
I hope you enjoyed it.
More to come...
Z.R.